What Ottoline Saw

Look out for Ottoline's paw mark. At the back of the book there is a description of what Ottoline really saw in the British Museum. You can see these things too, except for the Feeding Place, which is only for wardens – and cats.

OTTOLINE
AT THE BRITISH MUSEUM

written by Sally Craddock
illustrated by Corinne Pearlman

Macdonald

Ottoline knew she was beautiful because
people were always telling her so.

She sat in the window of her London house,
and even strangers would stop outside
to admire her long white fur and blue eyes.

But it was a lonely life because
she never saw any other cats –

except the Orange Hisser.

He sat on the garden wall and spat at her.

On the other side of this wall
there was a huge house, with lots of windows
and tall white pillars.
All day long, people went up and down the steps.
Ottoline thought they all lived there,
so perhaps some friendly cats lived there too.

One afternoon, when the Orange Hisser wasn't around,
Ottoline jumped over the wall.
Nobody noticed her sneaking up the wide, white steps.

Nobody saw her hiding behind one of the tall, white pillars. So she just slipped in through the door when it opened.

Inside, the walls were so high
she couldn't see the top.

All around her were legs –

boots

shoes

sandals

ankles

toes

but no paws.

Ottoline crept through to another room.

Suddenly she saw the most gigantic cat.
Its great mouth was open, as if roaring,
but no sound came out.

Ottoline's fur stood on end,
but none of the people in the room
took any notice.

Perhaps it's only yawning,
thought Ottoline.
But she hurried past all the same.

Further on, there were two people with friendly cat faces.
They seemed to be patting their laps
and asking her to jump up.
But she knew she would slide off their
hard shiny skirts. Ottoline preferred
somewhere soft to curl up.

‘Let’s go and see the mummies,’ somebody said.
That sounded interesting because
Ottoline was beginning to feel hungry.
Perhaps one of the mummies would give her some food.

So she followed the people upstairs
past a picture of fish on a dish,
which was a very good sign.

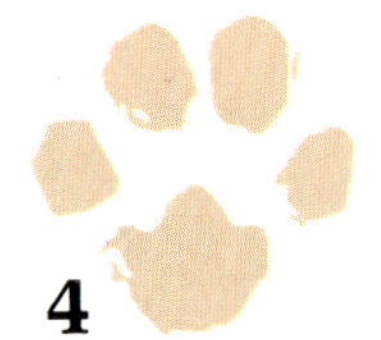

4

'Here we are,' the people said.
But there was no fish, no milk,
not even a tin opener in sight.
There were some cats though!
They were sitting on shelves, in rows.
Ottoline rushed up to talk to them and bang!
Her nose hit cold glass.
The cats didn't move. They couldn't move.
They were all bandaged up and their eyes were empty.
'Those cats have been dead for thousands of years,'
somebody whispered.

Ottoline felt very frightened.
Who put all those cats into glass boxes?

Ottoline didn't want to be caught like that,
so she hid in a dark corner.

Suddenly a voice called,
'The galleries are closing now.'
Ottoline was too scared to move
until everybody had gone.
Then she realized – she didn't know the way out.

There were so many doors and so many rooms
and they all looked the same.

She ran and ran until round a corner –

she saw a long line of people in blue uniforms.
They each carried a big bunch of keys.

These are the ones who locked up the cats, thought Ottoline, and she turned tail and fled.

From far away she heard voices echoing,
'Good night, Rex.' 'See you tomorrow, Lil.'
Then the whole place went quiet.
She was on her own, shut in.
Suddenly all the lights went out.

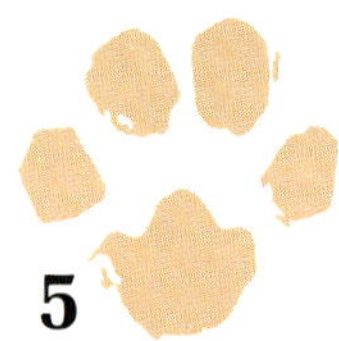

And, out of the darkness, she heard
a comforting, purring, whirring sound.
5 She crept towards it very slowly.

The cat-like sound got louder and louder.
Prrr *Prrr* PRRR, tick tock *tick tock* TICK TOCK.
All around her were ghostly faces with numbers on them,
leering and looming and laughing at her.
BOOM! CRASH! BOOM!
All the clocks chimed together.

Ottoline shot out of that room so fast that her paws hardly touched the ground. With a flying leap she jumped into a tree.

Well, Ottoline thought it was a tree,
but it had no leaves and no branches.
She slithered down to the ground
right in front of –

7

a great sea of breathing, screaming,
purring, fighting, jostling,
real live cats.

They swept her along with them
in a glorious wave of fur,
right out through a door and into the fresh air.

And there, under a notice saying
Authorized Cat Feeding Place,
stood one of the men in uniform.
He didn't seem at all frightening now because
he was dishing out bowls of delicious cat food.

'Hello,' he said. 'You're new. Come on – tuck in.'
And who do you think shared his bowl with Ottoline?
Why – the Orange Hisser himself.
Only he wasn't hissing now. He was purring –
and so was she.

This is the British Museum, her new friends told her.
Everybody is welcome here. Always.

AUTHORIZED
CAT FEEDING
PLACE

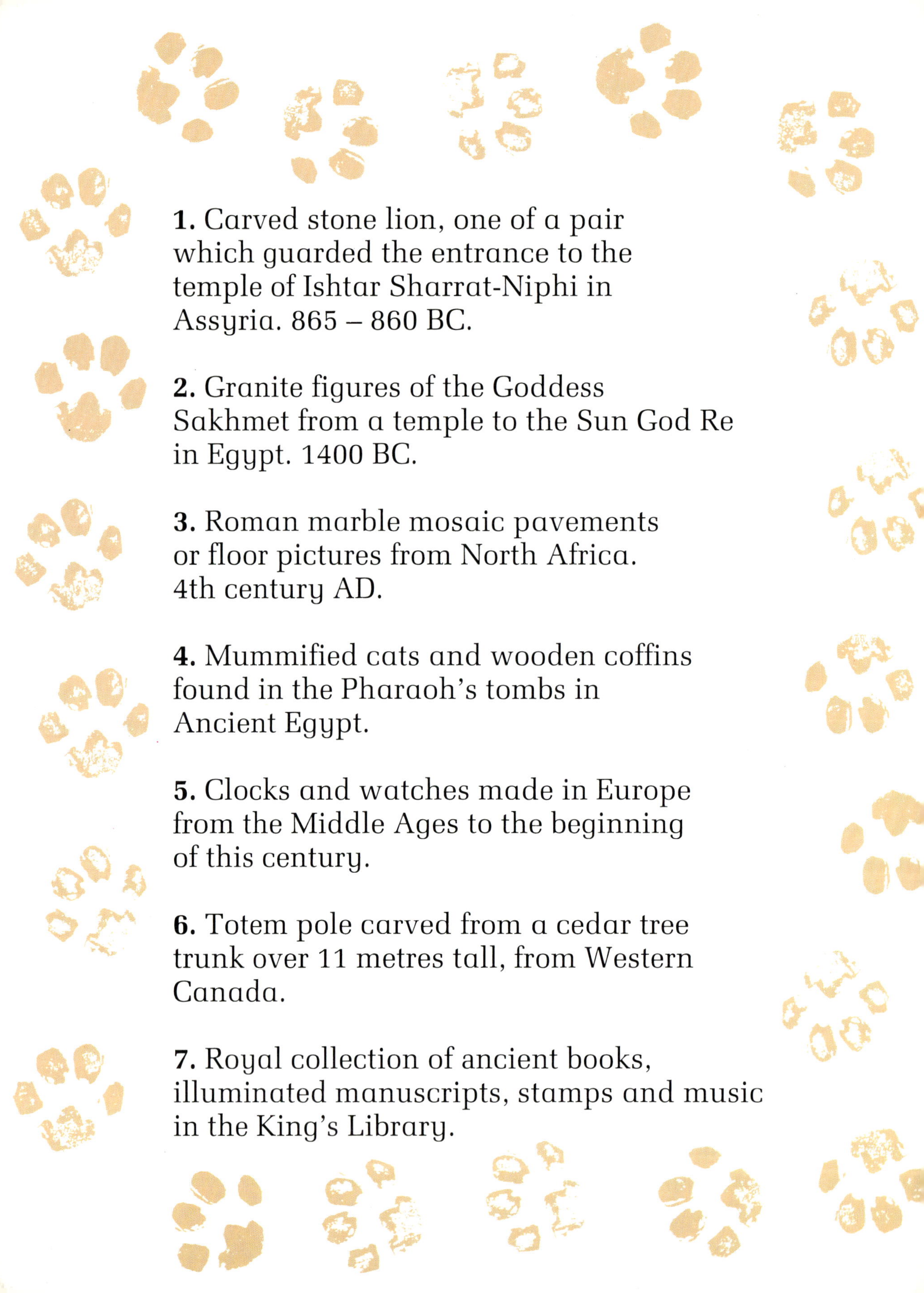

1. Carved stone lion, one of a pair which guarded the entrance to the temple of Ishtar Sharrat-Niphi in Assyria. 865 – 860 BC.

2. Granite figures of the Goddess Sakhmet from a temple to the Sun God Re in Egypt. 1400 BC.

3. Roman marble mosaic pavements or floor pictures from North Africa. 4th century AD.

4. Mummified cats and wooden coffins found in the Pharaoh's tombs in Ancient Egypt.

5. Clocks and watches made in Europe from the Middle Ages to the beginning of this century.

6. Totem pole carved from a cedar tree trunk over 11 metres tall, from Western Canada.

7. Royal collection of ancient books, illuminated manuscripts, stamps and music in the King's Library.

A MACDONALD BOOK

First published in Great Britain in 1987
by Macdonald & Co (Publishers) Ltd
London & Sydney
A BPCC plc company

Printed and bound in Great Britain by
Purnell Book Production Limited
Member of BPCC Group

Macdonald & Co (Publishers) Ltd
Greater London House
Hampstead Road
London NW1 7QX

British Library Cataloguing in Publication Data
Craddock, Sally
Ottoline at the British Museum. —
(Picture book fiction)
I. Title II. Pearlman, Corinne III. Series
823'.914 [J] PZ7

ISBN 0-356-11783-9
ISBN 0-356-11784-7 Pbk